8 93

THE AMAZING FACT BOOK OF

PLANES

by ROSALIND LENGA

**Illustrated by
Roy Coombs**

A & P/Creative Education

Contents

A & P BOOKS
8105 Edgewater Dr.
Oakland, CA 94621
A division of
The Atlantic & Pacific Commerce Co., Inc.

Library of Congress Catalog Card No. 80–80619
Illustrations Copyright © 1973 The Archon Press Limited
Text Copyright © 1979 Franklin Watts Limited
First published in USA by A & P Books 1980
Hardbound edition distributed by Creative Education, Inc., Mankato, MN

ISBN 0–86550–006–1 Hardbound (Volume 4)
ISBN 0–86550–007–X Softbound (Volume 4)
ISBN 0–86550–024–X Hardbound (12 Volume Set)
ISBN 0–86550–024–8 Softbound (12 Volume Set)

Printed in USA by Worzalla Publishing Co.

21,562

Introduction

For thousands of years man has envied the birds' freedom of the sky, and has dreamed of being able to fly. An early Greek legend tells how Icarus and Daedelus tried to escape from the Island of Crete by flying with wings made of bird feathers and stuck to their arms with wax.

In the 1500's the author and sculptor Leonardo da Vinci drew plans for a flying machine. Although it was never built, scientists today believe that, given suitable power, his machine could have flown. However, although the ideas were there, it was not until the beginning of the twentieth century that science and technology were far enough advanced to lead to the science of aerodynamics, and provide the "know-how" for a light and powerful engine, and suitable construction and control. With the Wrights' Flyer I of 1903, man's conquest of the air had begun.

This historic feat was followed by a surge of enthusiasm resulting in the production of some incredible – yet marvellously inventive – aircraft, particularly in France. Another turning point in the development of aircraft was World War I. By 1918 planes were efficient and effective fighters as well as flying machines.

From these first years when speeds were no greater than 48 k.p.h. (30 m.p.h.) and distances covered were measured in meters, man has created planes that fly higher, faster and longer than the Wright Brothers could ever have dreamed possible. It is hard to realize that the invention of the airplane spans no more than a lifetime, and that from the first frail plane – in the air for just 12 seconds – the huge Skycrane and the supersonic Concorde have developed.

Trouvé Ornithopter

Many early inventors of flying craft looked to birds for inspiration. A Frenchman, Gustave Trouvé, reasoned that, if birds could fly, then – with the aid of machines – so could man. His ingenious ornithopter of 1870, with its two flapping wings, imitated birds in flight. At the top was a canopy which could be moved up or down. This model machine actually propelled itself an amazing 61 m (200 ft).

Origin: France.

Size: Model-size only.

Mechanism: The wings were worked by blank revolver cartridges automatically fired into a tube. The cartridge forced down the wings, while the spring action of the tube brought them up again – ready for the next shot.

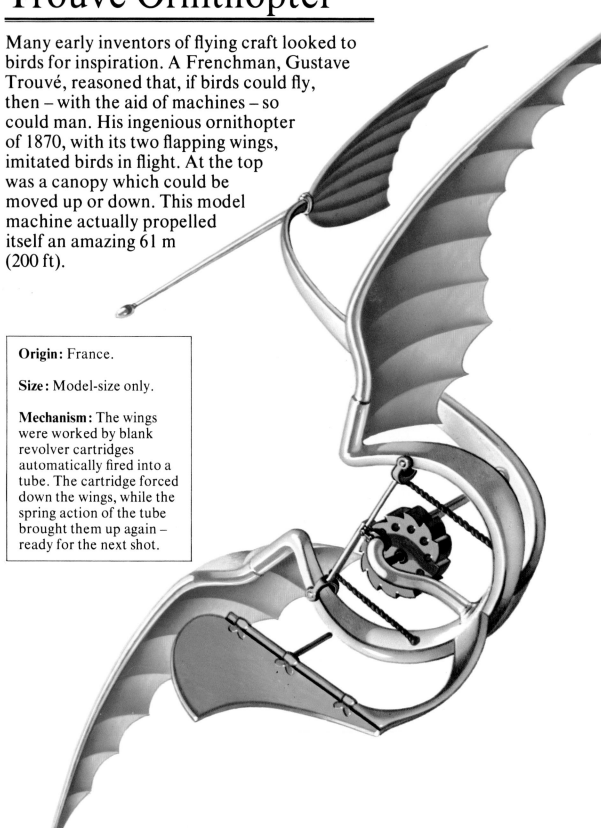

Du Temple's Plane

After experimenting for many years with models, Felix du Temple's plane of 1874 made the first successful powered flight in history. His plane, piloted by a young sailor, took off by running down a ramp before making a short hop in the air. It probably had a steam engine, which would have been too heavy for a sustained flight.

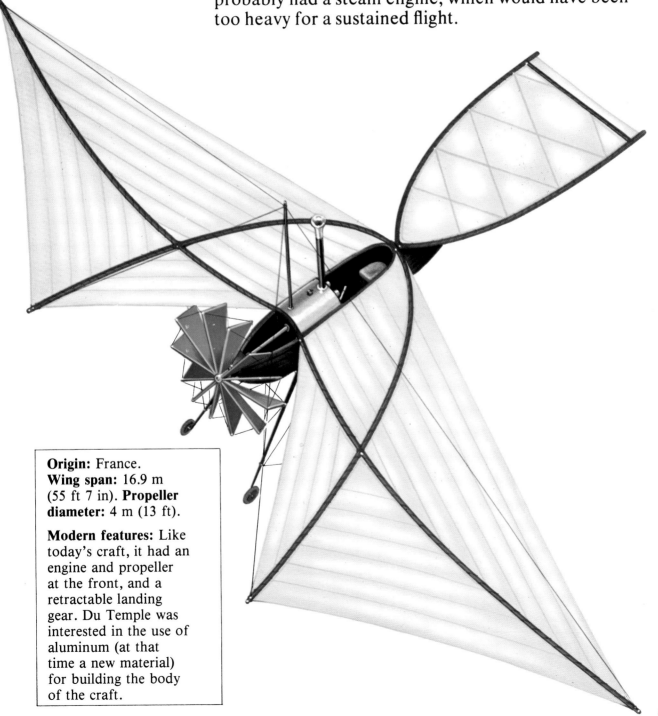

Origin: France.
Wing span: 16.9 m (55 ft 7 in). **Propeller diameter:** 4 m (13 ft).

Modern features: Like today's craft, it had an engine and propeller at the front, and a retractable landing gear. Du Temple was interested in the use of aluminum (at that time a new material) for building the body of the craft.

Wright Flyer I

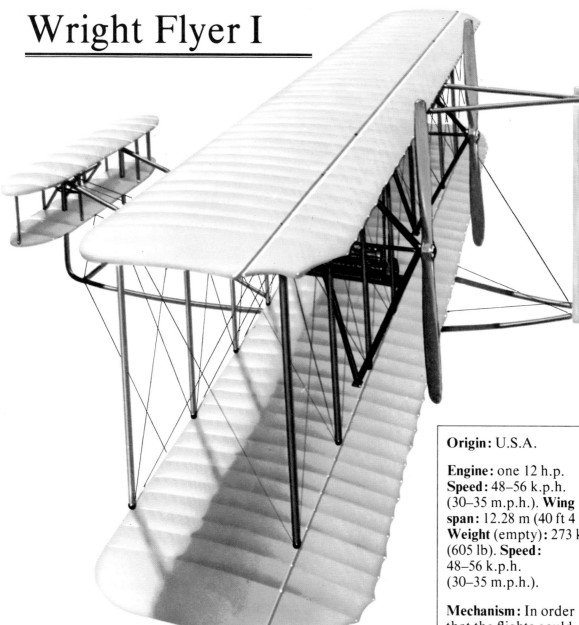

Origin: U.S.A.

Engine: one 12 h.p.
Speed: 48–56 k.p.h.
(30–35 m.p.h.). **Wing
span:** 12.28 m (40 ft 4 in).
Weight (empty): 273 kg
(605 lb). **Speed:**
48–56 k.p.h.
(30–35 m.p.h.).

Mechanism: In order
that the flights could
take place, the Wright
brothers both designed
and helped build the
engine and propeller –
the first of their kind.

Wings: Much of the
success was due to the
innovation of wing
warping: by moving the
free ends of wings the
pilot could change
direction and increase
stability.

After many experiments with gliders, the American
brothers Wilbur and Orville Wright built the first
plane ever to achieve true flight. This historic
moment took place on 17 December, 1903, at Kitty
Hawk, North Carolina, when Flyer I flew for 12
seconds and 36.5 m (120 ft). Strangely enough, this
historic occasion was given little attention by the
American public and, for a while, most of the early
pioneering in aviation took place on the other side
of the Atlantic.

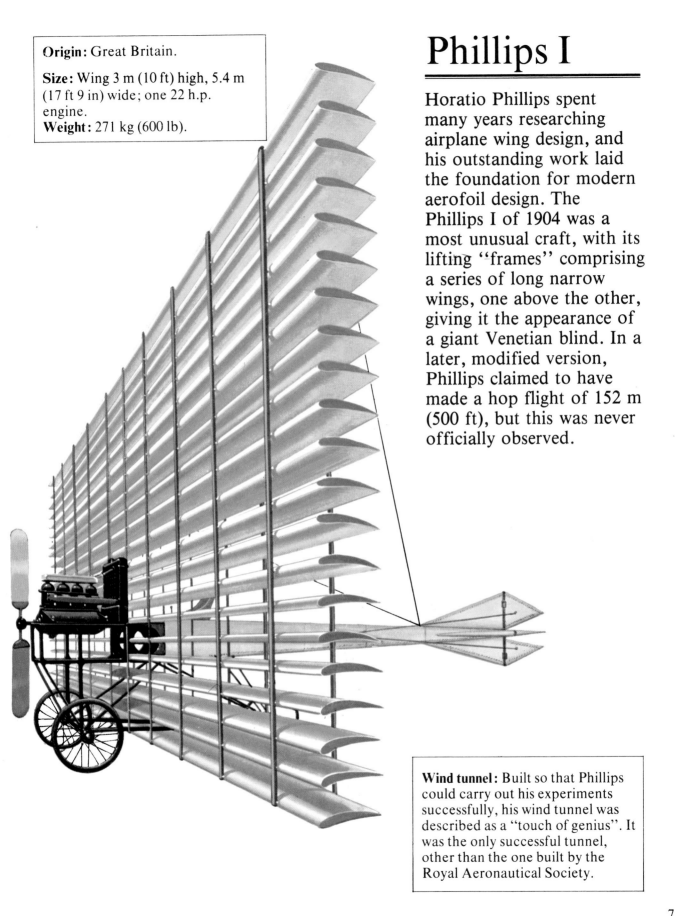

Origin: Great Britain.

Size: Wing 3 m (10 ft) high, 5.4 m (17 ft 9 in) wide; one 22 h.p. engine.
Weight: 271 kg (600 lb).

Phillips I

Horatio Phillips spent many years researching airplane wing design, and his outstanding work laid the foundation for modern aerofoil design. The Phillips I of 1904 was a most unusual craft, with its lifting "frames" comprising a series of long narrow wings, one above the other, giving it the appearance of a giant Venetian blind. In a later, modified version, Phillips claimed to have made a hop flight of 152 m (500 ft), but this was never officially observed.

Wind tunnel: Built so that Phillips could carry out his experiments successfully, his wind tunnel was described as a "touch of genius". It was the only successful tunnel, other than the one built by the Royal Aeronautical Society.

Vuia Number I

Origin: France
(Vuia was Hungarian
by birth).
Wing span: 8.7 m
(28 ft 7 in).
Weight: 240 kg
(531 lb).

Trajan Vuia built the first conventionally-shaped monoplane in history. The bat-shaped wings were controlled by wires. Vuia made several hop flights in 1906, the best being 24 m (80 ft). His Number II monoplane of 1907 was less successful and shortly afterwards he gave up his work in aviation.

Design: The four-wheeled undercarriage has the unique distinction of being the first with pneumatic-tired wheels.

Ellehammer II

The strange-looking Ellehammer II was a semi bi-plane invented by the Dane, Jacob Christian Ellehammer. He claimed to have made the first manned flight in Europe but, in fact, his plane was tethered by a wire to a central post. Although he made a hop flight of 41 m (137 ft), it could not be considered a free flight. Ellehammer built this plane in 1906.

Origin: Denmark.

Speed: 56 k.p.h. (35 m.p.h.).
Wing span: 9.43 m (30 ft 11¾ in), 3.26 m (10 ft 8¾ in) high.
Weight: 179 kg (397 lb).

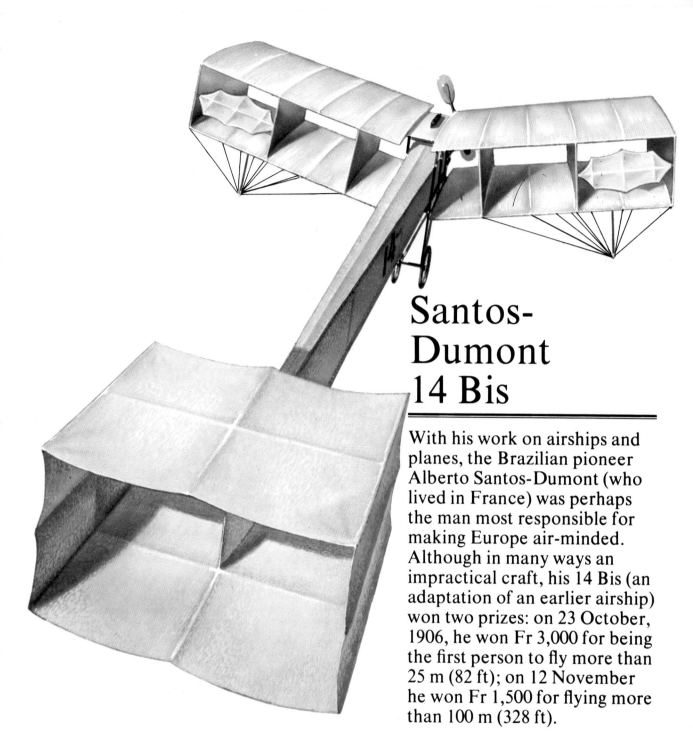

Santos-Dumont 14 Bis

With his work on airships and planes, the Brazilian pioneer Alberto Santos-Dumont (who lived in France) was perhaps the man most responsible for making Europe air-minded. Although in many ways an impractical craft, his 14 Bis (an adaptation of an earlier airship) won two prizes: on 23 October, 1906, he won Fr 3,000 for being the first person to fly more than 25 m (82 ft); on 12 November he won Fr 1,500 for flying more than 100 m (328 ft).

Origin: France.
Length: 9.6 m (31 ft 10 in).
Wing span: 11.1 m (36 ft 9 in).
Weight: 299 kg (661 lb).
Flight: On 23 October he flew 60 m (197 ft); on 12 November he flew 220 m (722 ft) in $21\frac{1}{3}$ seconds, at a speed of 41.05 k.p.h. (25.496 m.p.h.), which won him fame as the first European to fly.

Flight position: Compared with modern aircraft his plane was "back to front", with its tail at the front and the propellor at the extreme tail end. However, he pioneered the development of ailerons, a more efficient version of the Wrights' wing-warping. It was probably an uncomfortable flight as the pilot had to stand up!

Santos-Dumont Demoiselle

Origin: France.
Wing-span: 5 m
(16 ft 5 in).
Weight: 109 kg (242 lb).
Speed: 40.25 k.p.h.
(25 m.p.h.).

After his success with the 14 Bis, Santos-Dumont abandoned the bi-plane in favor of the monoplane. In 1907 he began building the first of a remarkable series of small light machines, later called the Demoiselle ("Dragonfly") because of their light and delicate design. Each machine was made of canvas with bamboo struts, and Santos-Dumont hoped it would be the first "do-it-yourself" aircraft kit. It did three hop flights, the longest being 199 m (654 ft) before crashing. Two years later, a more successful version stayed in the air for 10 minutes. The Demoiselle was the first successful monoplane.

Blériot XI

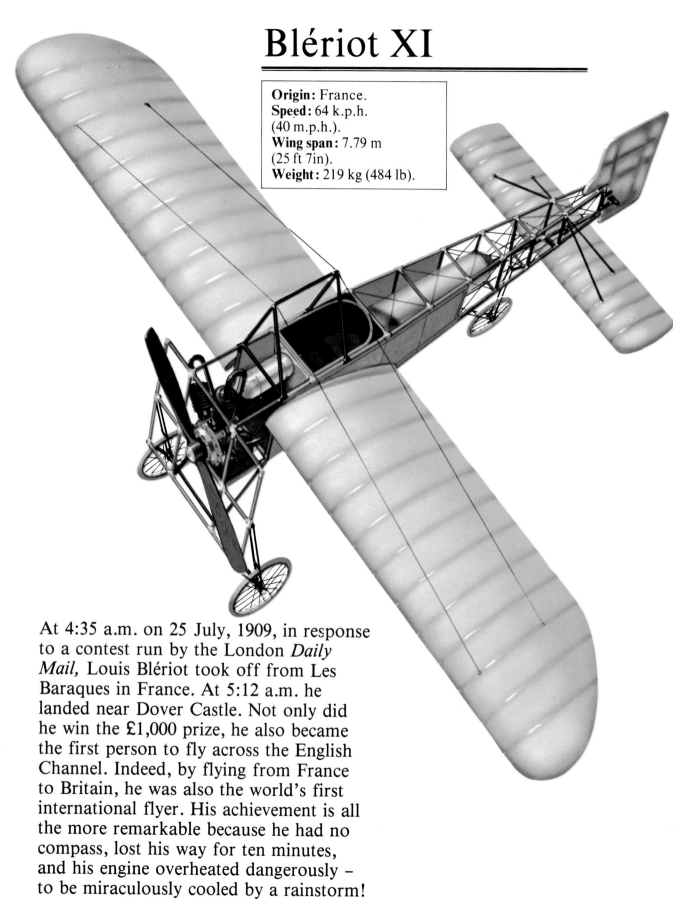

Origin: France.
Speed: 64 k.p.h.
(40 m.p.h.).
Wing span: 7.79 m
(25 ft 7in).
Weight: 219 kg (484 lb).

At 4:35 a.m. on 25 July, 1909, in response to a contest run by the London *Daily Mail,* Louis Blériot took off from Les Baraques in France. At 5:12 a.m. he landed near Dover Castle. Not only did he win the £1,000 prize, he also became the first person to fly across the English Channel. Indeed, by flying from France to Britain, he was also the world's first international flyer. His achievement is all the more remarkable because he had no compass, lost his way for ten minutes, and his engine overheated dangerously – to be miraculously cooled by a rainstorm!

Fabre Seaplane Hydravion

Origin: France.
Speed: 88 k.p.h.
(55 m.p.h.).
Wing span: 13.9 m
(45 ft 11 in).
Weight: 473 kg
(1,047 lb).

Floats: Like most
machines operating from
water, the Hydravion
had floats, which
provided lift from the
water and assisted in
supporting the craft in
the air.

One of the problems with the early planes was taking off from rough, bumpy ground. Henri Fabre, the son of a French shipbuilder, decided to construct a seaplane as water offered a much gentler "taking-off" surface. On 28 March, 1910, near Marseilles, Fabre became the first person to take off successfully from the sea, and his plane flew for several miles. However, although he could take off from water, he needed a sandy beach or grass meadow for landing.

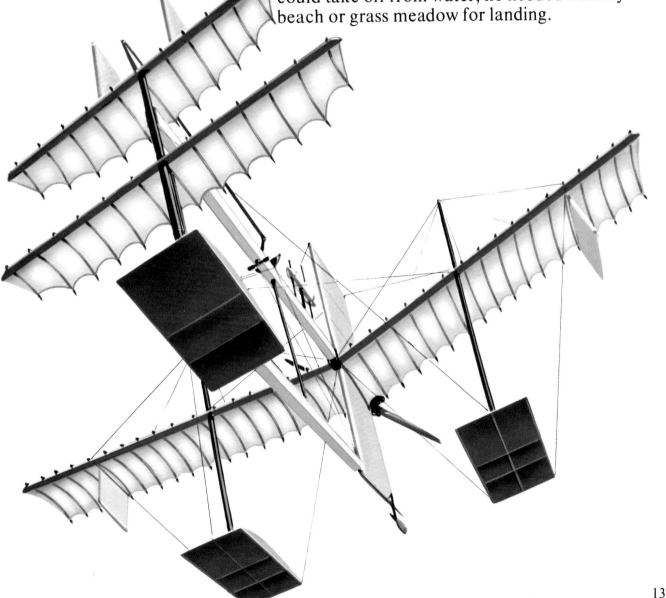

Sikorsky "Le Grand"

The Russian Igor Sikorsky's "Le Grand" of 1913 broke many "firsts". It was the first passenger-carrying aircraft ever built, and the largest heavier-than-air craft of its time. It was first known as "Bolsche" (Russian for "great"), but it is now known by its French name. As Sikorsky could not find wheels big enough, the undercarriage had sixteen wheels. It was the first four-engined plane to fly and the first plane to have a furnished passenger cabin. It first flew on 13 May 1913 (for 10 minutes), but on 2 August it flew for two hours. This plane made 50 flights before being damaged by an engine falling from a crashing plane. Shortly afterwards Sikorsky fled from Russia for America, where he became famous for building helicopters (see page 27).

Origin: Russia.
Engine: four 100 h.p. 4-cylinder Argus water-cooled.
Speed: 88 k.p.h. (55 m.p.h.).
Length: 20 m (65 ft 8 in).
Weight: 2,692 kg (5,950 lb).

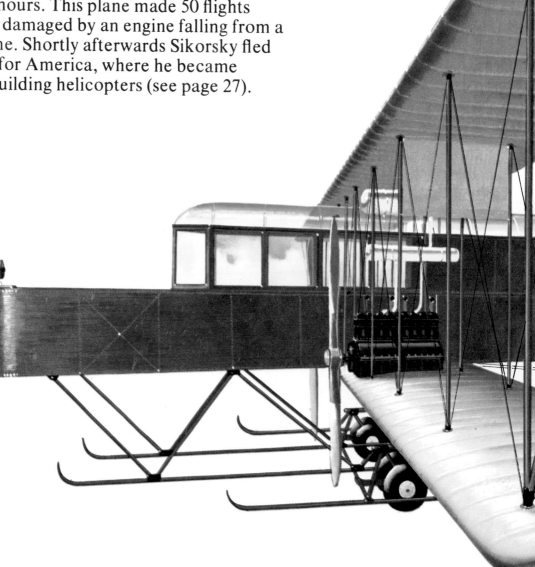

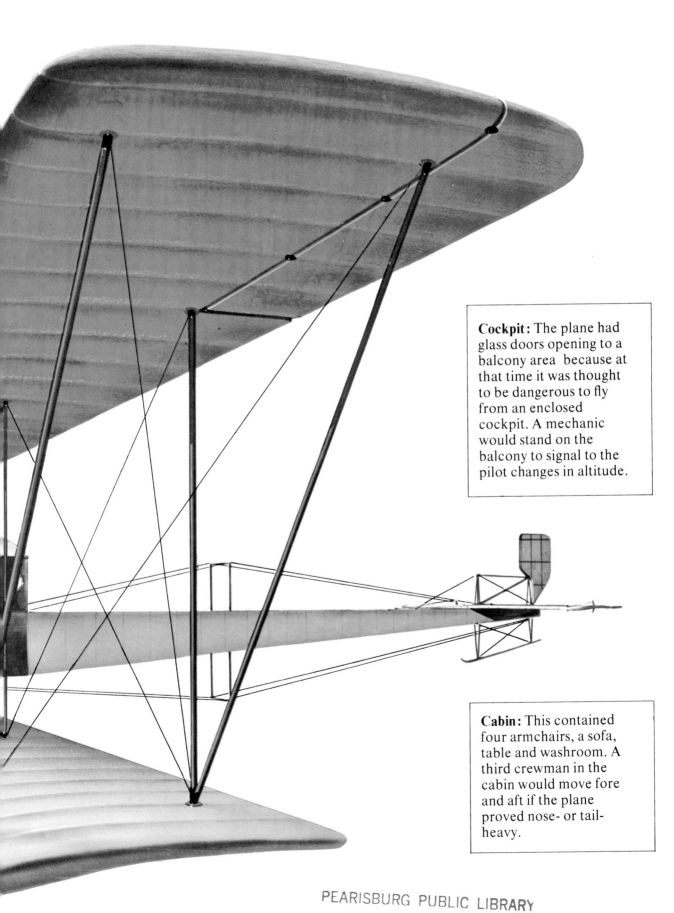

Cockpit: The plane had glass doors opening to a balcony area because at that time it was thought to be dangerous to fly from an enclosed cockpit. A mechanic would stand on the balcony to signal to the pilot changes in altitude.

Cabin: This contained four armchairs, a sofa, table and washroom. A third crewman in the cabin would move fore and aft if the plane proved nose- or tail-heavy.

15

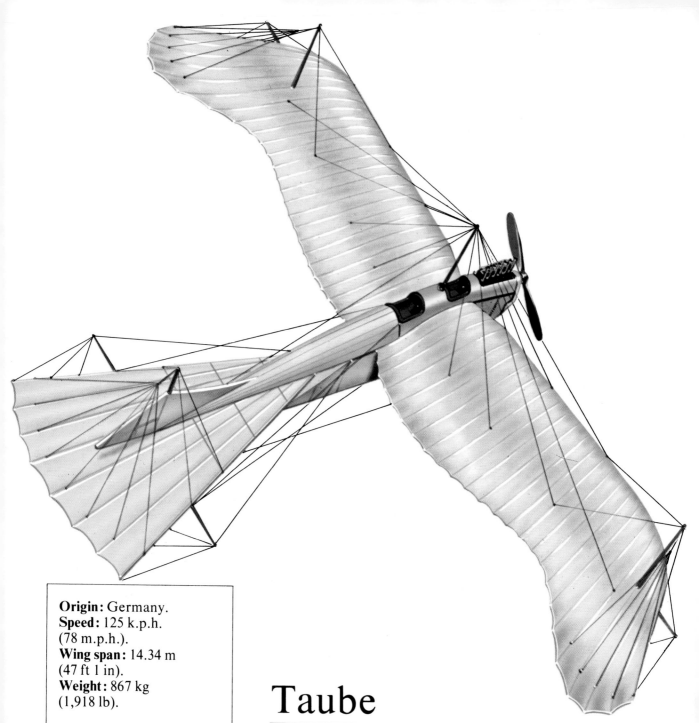

Origin: Germany.
Speed: 125 k.p.h.
(78 m.p.h.).
Wing span: 14.34 m
(47 ft 1 in).
Weight: 867 kg
(1,918 lb).

Sale of copyright:
Etrich's Austrian
government turned
down the design, but he
was approached by a
German secret service
agent to whom he sold
the design. Shortly
afterwards he retired
from the world of
aviation.

Taube

Although Igo Etrich called his brilliant plane of
1912 "Taube" (German for "dove") because of
its bird-like appearance, he actually got his
inspiration from the falling wing-shaped seeds
of a palm tree. Watching the seeds fall, Etrich
was sure the movement could be translated into
aeronautical design. This graceful plane was to
develop into a very efficient World War I
reconnaissance plane.

Opel Rocket Plane

In the 1920's aircraft engineers experimented with rocket propulsion as a means of powering aircraft. In 1928 some German engineers, including Fritz von Opel, successfully built such a craft, but it was damaged on landing. The project was abandoned. Opel, however, decided to carry on with the experiments and in 1929 successfully piloted the world's first "jet" aeroplane.

Take-off: The plane was catapulted from a cradle and, once it was airborne, the rockets were fired. At one point the plane reached 161 k.p.h. (100 m.p.h.).

Origin: Germany.

Wing span: 16.9 m (55 ft 8 in).

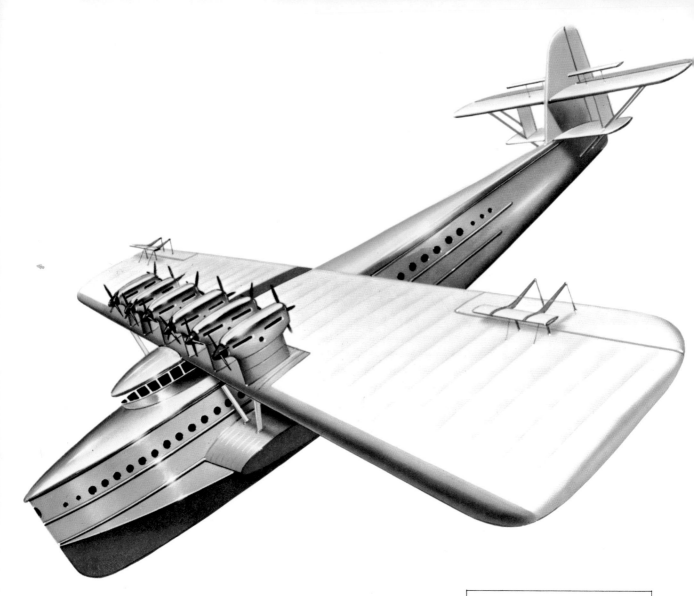

Dornier DO X

When it appeared in 1929, Dornier's enormous flying boat, the DO X, was the world's largest airplane ever built, comparable in size to today's jumbo jets. It could carry up to 170 passengers (most aircraft at that time carried 20). In 1931 it took 100 passengers and 10 crew by easy stages from Lisbon to Brazil to New York, returning to Germany nearly a year later.

Origin: Germany.

Engine: Twelve 600 h.p. water-cooled Curtiss Conquerors.
Speed: 215 k.p.h. (134 m.p.h.).
Wing span: 47.9 m (157 ft 5 in).
Weight (empty): 29,429 kg (65,040 lb).

Seaplane: Even with twelve engines, the Dornier DO X was underpowered for lengthy flights, so on long ocean journeys it could skim over the surface of the water.

Origin: Great Britain.

Warplane: The technical knowledge gleaned from the S6B laid the foundations for Britain's finest World War II fighter, the Spitfire.

Wing span: 9.13 m (30 ft).
Weight: 2,063 kg (4,560 lb).
Speed: The S6B flew the race at 548 k.p.h. (340.4 m.p.h.). A second machine raised the world speed record to 659.2 k.p.h. (409.5 m.p.h.).

Supermarine S6B

In 1913, to encourage the development of marine aviation, the French arms manufacturer, Jacques Schneider, offered a trophy to the winner of a tough air race. Any country to win three times in succession could keep it. Britain won in 1927, and also in 1929, with the Supermarine SB. Supermarine entered the S6B for the 1931 race – which they won, so that the trophy now belongs to Britain.

Origin: Great Britain.
Engines: *Maia*: Four
960 h.p. Bristol Pegasus X
engines.
Mercury: Four 395 h.p.
Bristol Pegasus engines.

Flight: This first two-stage
aircraft made a new
record "non-stop" flight
of 6,000 miles (10,000 km)
from Scotland to South
Africa.

Mayo
Composite

The Mayo Composite of
1938 had an ingenious way
of coping with trans-
Atlantic travel. The
Maia, a large aircraft,
was built for the take-off,
while the smaller
Mercury, which was
carried "piggy-back"
fashion for part of the way across the
Atlantic, was launched in mid-air
with enough fuel to complete the
journey.

GB Sportster

The "golden age" of American air races, the 1930's, produced one of the most spectacular aircraft of all time. Designed specifically for air racing, the Gee Bees were a combination of the largest engine and the smallest body. The most famous of all, the R-1 *(above)* enjoyed a brief, but glorious, history. It won the much-coveted Thompson Trophy Race in 1932, but in 1933, when competing in the Bendix Trophy race, it suddenly went out of control and crashed upside down.

Origin: U.S.A.

Wing span: 7.6 m (25 ft).
Speed: It set a new land plane speed record of 477 k.p.h. (296.287 m.p.h.).
Weight: 832 kg (1,840 lb).

R–2: This later plane met a similar fate and the remains of the R–1 and R–2 were pieced together to form the R–1/R–2, another formidable racer. This crashed in 1935 while racing, and so ended the amazing racing history of the Gee Bees.

Pou-de-Ciel

Nicknamed the "flying flea", the Pou-de-Ciel was the ninth of a series of light aircraft designs produced by the Frenchman, Henri Mignet. With the details publicized as a "do-it-yourself" exercise, this plane soon became very popular. By the end of 1935, over 100 had been privately built, and a series of "Pou" clubs formed. But several fatal accidents brought this success to a rapid halt as an inquiry showed that there was a basic defect in the aircraft's design.

Origin: France.
Wing span: 5.9 m (19 ft 7 in).
Speed: 99 k.p.h. (62 m.p.h.).
Weight: 99.5 kg (220 lb).

Seating: This monoplane was unique in that the pilot sat underneath the wing.

Origin: U.S.A.

Wing span: 43 m (141 ft 3 in).

Weight: 65,610 kg (145,000 lb).

Fuselage: Up to 7.6 m

(25 ft) in diameter. The nose is hinged so that it can swing open for easy loading.

Aero Spacelines B-377, Super Guppy

Possibly the world's most ugly aircraft, this plane was developed from the Boeing Strato-cruiser C97 to transport the huge stages of American space rockets. The Super Guppy was developed entirely with private money, and the United States Government then contracted for the exclusive use of the aircraft. It first flew in August 1965, and even today it is still the world's largest aircraft.

Cornu Helicopter

Helicopters have their origins in the "helicopter toys" made by the ancient Chinese. In the 1500's Leonardo da Vinci produced a design which, theoretically, was very sound. However, it was the Frenchman, Paul Cornu who, in 1907, built the "flying bicycle" – the first helicopter ever to fly freely.

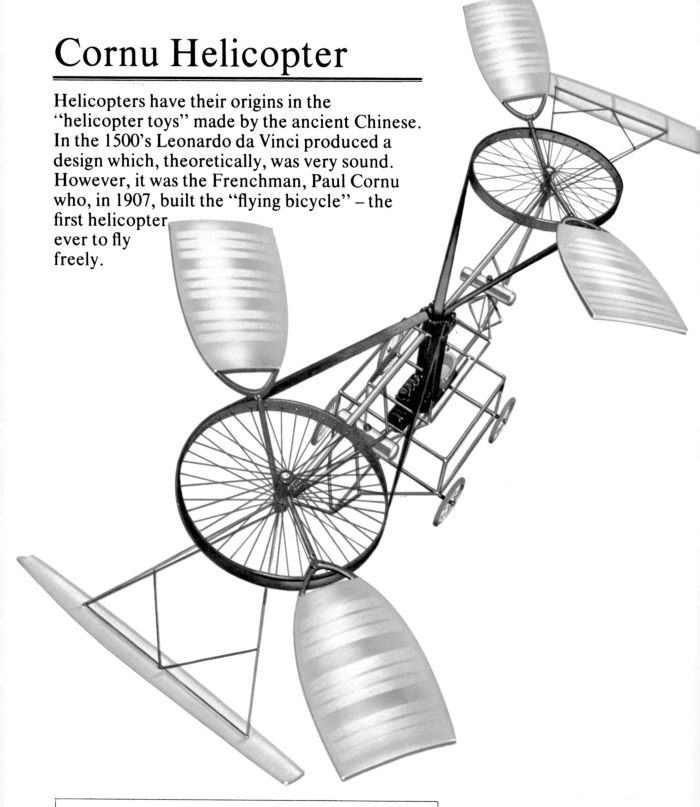

Origin: France.

Length: 12 m (40 ft).
Rotors: 6.19 m (20 ft 4 in) diameter.

Future: Although Cornu pioneered the development of helicopters, they were not very successful until the 1930's.

Origin: U.S.A.
Speed: 188 k.p.h.
(117 m.p.h.).
Length: 26.95 m (88 ft 6 in).
Weight: 19,004 kg
(42,000 lb).

Sikorsky
S-64 Skycrane

Although helicopters are uneconomic for long-distance travel, they are unequalled for lifting heavy goods. The S–64, one of the world's largest helicopters, has flown higher with a greater load than any other helicopter.

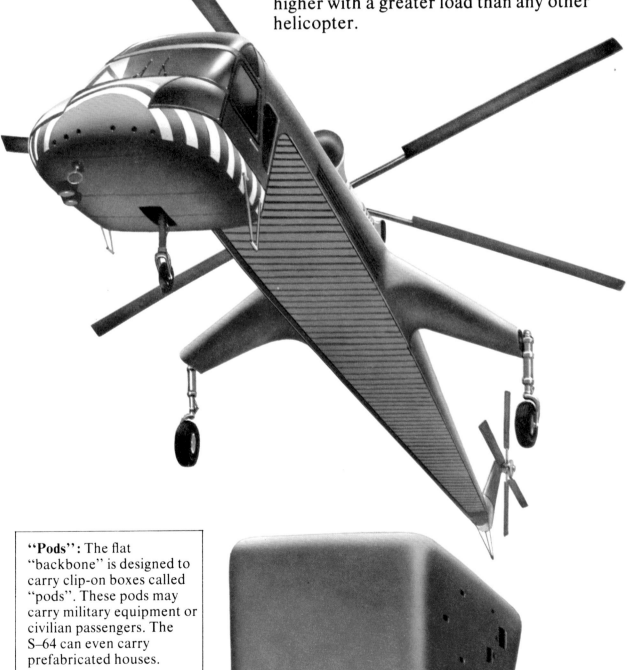

"Pods": The flat "backbone" is designed to carry clip-on boxes called "pods". These pods may carry military equipment or civilian passengers. The S–64 can even carry prefabricated houses.

27

Rolls-Royce TMR
Flying Bedstead

This ungainly craft was built as a prototype for VTOL (vertical take-off and landing) craft, and was a forerunner of the spectacular Harrier jump jet. The thin undercarriage legs had shock absorbers to save the pilot if the engine failed.

Origin: Great Britain.

Span: 4.26 m (14 ft).
Length: 8.53 m (28 ft).
Height: 4.5 m (15 ft).
Weight: 3,256 kg (7,196 lb).

Power: It was lifted by a series of nozzles which directed the thrust of the jet engines towards the ground. The pilot controlled the nozzles to keep it level.

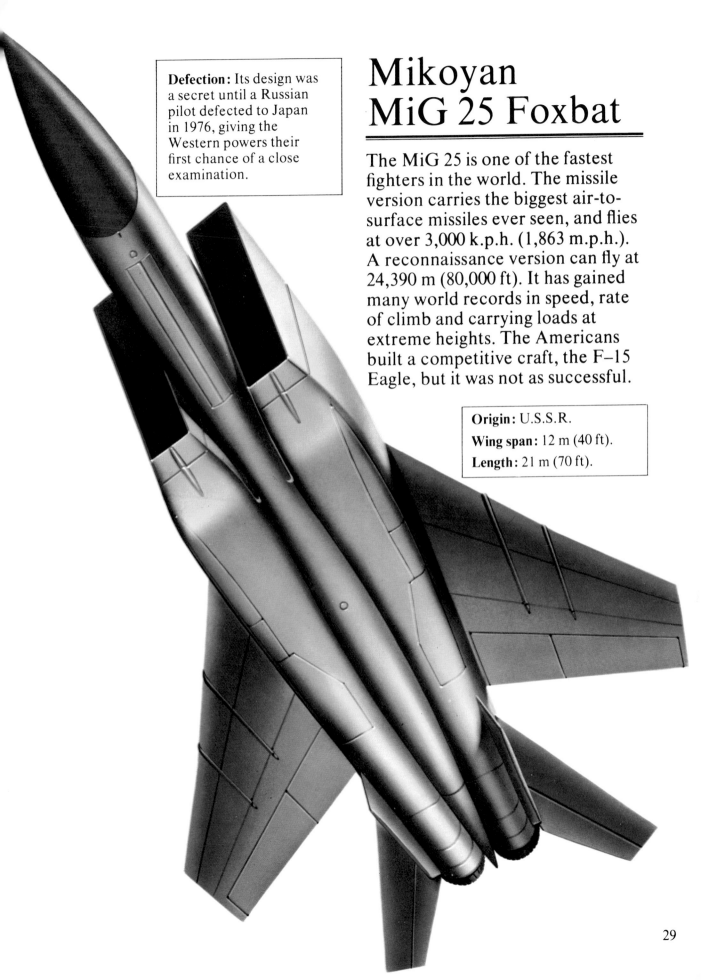

Defection: Its design was a secret until a Russian pilot defected to Japan in 1976, giving the Western powers their first chance of a close examination.

Mikoyan MiG 25 Foxbat

The MiG 25 is one of the fastest fighters in the world. The missile version carries the biggest air-to-surface missiles ever seen, and flies at over 3,000 k.p.h. (1,863 m.p.h.). A reconnaissance version can fly at 24,390 m (80,000 ft). It has gained many world records in speed, rate of climb and carrying loads at extreme heights. The Americans built a competitive craft, the F–15 Eagle, but it was not as successful.

Origin: U.S.S.R.
Wing span: 12 m (40 ft).
Length: 21 m (70 ft).

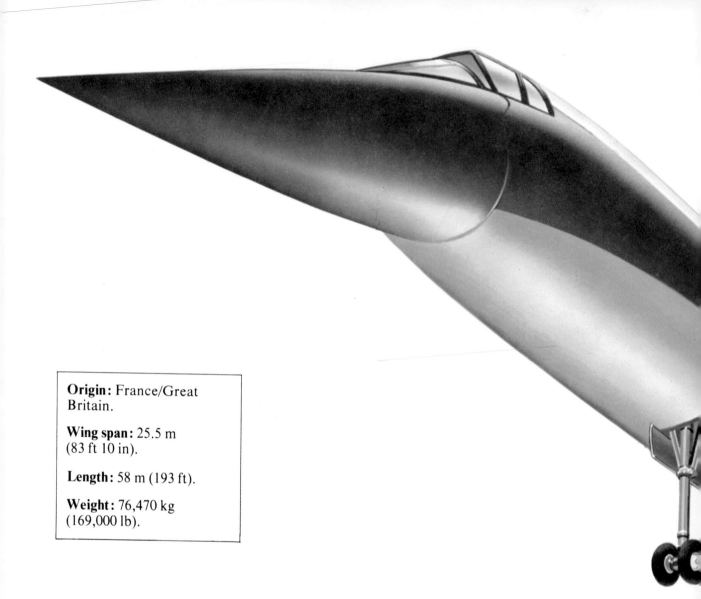

Origin: France/Great Britain.

Wing span: 25.5 m (83 ft 10 in).

Length: 58 m (193 ft).

Weight: 76,470 kg (169,000 lb).

Concorde

The most exciting development in civil aviation in recent years, Concorde is a joint development of Britain and France. It entered the service of British Airways and Air France in January 1976 to provide the world's first long-range supersonic passenger air service, carrying up to 128 passengers.

Its streamlined shape has many important features. Its nose section is lowered hydraulically on take-off and landing, which gives the pilot a better view of the runway.

The wings are specially designed for ultra-efficient cruising. There is a disadvantage in that it needs a very long runway for take-off and landing but, once it has taken off, it climbs so rapidly that engine noise lasts only for a few seconds.

Speed: It cruises at 2,179.9 k.p.h. (1,354 m.p.h.) at a height of 15,635 m (51,300 ft). The time of trans-Atlantic flying has been cut by nearly half.

Testing: It is the most thoroughly tested airliner in aeronautical history. It completed 5,000 hours of flying time before receiving a certificate of airworthiness, and a further 1,000 hours of testing on major airline routes.

Fuel: It can carry 118,300 liters (26,000 gallons) of fuel for a maximum range of 7,084 km (4,400 miles), while keeping enough in reserve for emergencies, e.g. delayed landing or diversion.

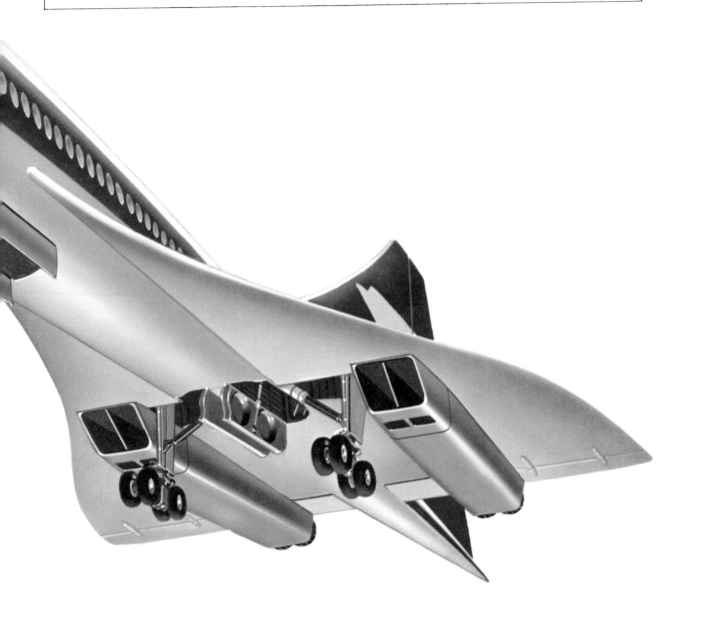

Glossary

aerodynamics: the designing of wings and bodies which cause the least resistance to lift.

aerofoil: curved section of a wing or rotor designed to produce lift.

aileron: hinged surfaces at trailing edges of wings for controlling rolling movement.

bi-plane: aircraft with two wings, one on top of the other.

fuselage: the body section of an aircraft.

horsepower (h.p.): unit of power equal to 550 footpounds, i.e. the energy required to propel 550 lb one foot – equivalent to 248 kg per 30 cm.

jet engine: engine which takes in air, heats it, expands it, and forcibly expels it from the rear of the engine, providing forward thrust (power).

monoplane: aircraft with one wing.

ornithopter: aircraft deriving its propulsion from flapping wings.

prototype: first model of any kind.